JACOB
(A FATHERLESS GENERATION)

by

Adrian L. Hawkes

*Foreword
&
Guest Chapter*

by

Chris Bulpitt

Rainbow Publishing

Rainbow Publishing
PO Box 17
Chichester
PO20 6YB

Other books by Adrian L. Hawkes

Leadership And...
Published by NLM Publications (first printing)
Published by New Wine Press
   (second edition/reprint)

Attracting, Training, Releasing Youth
Published by New Wine Press

Books by Gareth Hawkes and Mark Yates
Pomery We Shall Replace Poetry
Published by Generation Resource Centre

ISBN 1 903725 17 8

Printed in England by Clays Ltd, St Ives plc.

CONTENTS

JACOB

CONTENTS

FOREWORD BY CHRIS BULPITT

I have known Adrian since 1996 and am really happy to write this Foreword and to collaborate with him by providing my own Guest Chapter. I can think of many occasions when Adrian and I have had time together chewing over the ideas contained in this book and desiring to see them outworked in the world that we live in. One of the things I love about Adrian is the way in which after having said something to him he will look quizzically and ask the simple question, 'Why?'

FOREWORD

This has provoked me and us to write this book and try to get across to a larger audience realities which are on one level actually very simple but on another level could be life- changing once engaged with.

I know one of Adrian's main desires is to see people seeking the Kingdom of God first, with a trust that Jesus will build the kind of church that He is looking for.

In order for this to happen the next generation or 'Jacob' generation needs to be released to influence in church and society now. They need to be released and empowered at every age to do and shape church in the way that expresses their heartbeat for Jesus and the future.

So... read on and **be warned** that, if believed and acted upon, this book could seriously change your life and the lives of many people around you.

Chris Bulpitt
Colne Valley Community Church
Colchester

JACOB

THANKS

To Pauline my wife for putting up with me sitting in front of the computer for too long. That thanks is probably due also to Joanne, who brought me tea, Feraina, Cloie, Jerry, Sylvie, Ian, and Lucy, who live with us and who wondered if I was still living there or had entered the computer!

THANKS

Special thanks to Ian Wedd who not only lives with us but also brought his proof reading skills to bear on this book.

To Chris Bulpitt and the Colne Valley Community Church for their experimentation.

Big thanks to the Rainbow lot, because they are really going for it and I see a lot of them and they really are putting into practice the Ethos behind the whole of this book.

Thanks also to Gareth Illya, alias Zippy, for the poetry, sorry, pomery.

THE REASONING BEHIND THIS BOOK

THE AUTHOR'S PREFACE

Around 1998, Pioneer, the network of church with which I am in relationship, had quite a few prophetic words about "releasing Jacob, and yet working with Abraham and Isaac". I also heard similar 'words,' 'aspirations,' in other church circles saying things like it's time for a three- generational push.

For those of you who are not used to such 'words' or prophetic utterances, perhaps such pressure could be interpreted as just wishful thinking, or maybe too much cheese at night, the aspirations of drunkards or for people with a slightly unsound mind.

However, in the circles that I moved such prophetic utterances were generally thought needing to be checked, and *(the possibility of too much cheese not being over ruled)* taken seriously.

And if you think about it, being accused of being drunk when you are not does put one in good company, for that was exactly the accusation that Peter and the Apostles were accused of at the beginning of the church age some 2000 years ago. From my point of view that's not such bad company.

If you think about it, going right back into history, well before the time of Christ, it is not unusual to find the older generation- 'ABRAHAM' for the sake of the illustration- being very irritated by 'JACOB' or the younger generation.

JACOB

Right back in the days of Yore you can find the Greek writers claiming that civilization was about to be destroyed because of the attitude / approach etc., etc., of the younger generation. So what has changed? Not a lot it seems!

Also if we look at history recent or far, what we often see taking place is 'rebellion,' at least that's what some would say. Others would say they are new discoveries, experimentation, and development. Whatever they say, these things lead to the divorce of the younger generation from the older, be that very old like Abraham, or less old like Isaac.

Jacob, well he leaves home, runs away, goes off to explore the world and see if he can discover it for himself, whatever it is.

Be that new business, new scientific discoveries, or maybe new spirituality. Who is to say Jacob will miss any of these things?

AUTHOR'S PREFACE

Forgive me for using the word Jacob all the time, I don't think this ought to be gender related, for it could just as easily be Joanne, female as well as male. The thing that strikes me is the generational conflict, so often observed.

Sometimes that conflict is 'polite,' sometimes more raucous, but nevertheless it's there.

Sadly I feel that many in the church as a whole have generally missed this message. Whilst I think some have tried, many have not even tried too capture the Jacob Agenda. Sadly many don't even see any reason as to why they should!

Too many Abrahams and Isaacs who were yet looking for their own fulfilment perhaps; maybe some were yet insecure.

And so Jacob left, not necessarily in terms of moving out, even of our churches, but certainly left in attitude, in involvement in the Abraham or Isaac Agenda. Certainly left mentally and attitude wise if not physically.

JACOB

So why have I written this book? Well speaking from the perspective of an Abrahams or the female of the same age, I think that there is a need to look (for my own benefit, hopefully for yours to) as to what is, or what should be Jacobs agenda, if such an agenda is so important.

Maybe to even get some Abrahams and Isaacs or that female equivalent on board if the Agenda is valuable.

Along the way, in this book, to have a look at the kind of culture that our new younger generation is growing up in. What kind of world is it that I and perhaps you are struggling to understand?

Perhaps along the way to inject a little Fatherly / Motherly wisdom, even some of the Grandfatherly or Grandmotherly kind.

AUTHOR'S PREFACE

I guess what I would really like to do is to say to that newer Generation: "Have a go, take the challenge, change the world, and grab an agenda", an agenda that says in the words of Jesus Christ of Nazareth, "that the will of God should be done on earth as it is in Heaven"!

That should bring a spat of Justice, Peace, Healing and Righteousness. **That's a worthwhile AGENDA!**

CHAPTER ONE

JACOB'S STORY

You can, of course find the story of Jacob in the book of Genesis, the first book of the Bible. It runs from Chapter 26 right through to chapter 49, almost half of this quite long book of the Bible.

The story is of a family, with lots of internal pressure and conflict. We can say *'oh but'!* "Their culture was different to ours" but even with a cursory look at the story one can see the pressures of jealousy, the conflict caused by not a few sexual relationships, culturally acceptable or not.

JACOB'S STORY

We can see sibling rivalry and jealousy. We can see parents putting children in wrong positions. We see conflict and ultimately the young Jacob fleeing from home, homeless. There are a lot of modern day equivalents if we look.

Jacob was a twin. Seems to me he was the arty one of the family. I guess he liked music, art, maybe he liked to sense things. Certainly he seems to have been the sensitive one; unusually, I guess, for those times, he liked to cook. Certainly that seems to have endeared him to his mother. His twin Esau was just the opposite. He was the outdoor man, loved hunting and partying. Seemed he was the one who would have gone to the pub with dad. Certainly dad appreciated him, and was often making excuses for him.

Even their names tell stories. Jacob can mean twister or usurper. He certainly seemed to be good at both from the Bible narrative. Esau could easily mean of the earth, or red, or faithless.

JACOB

He certainly seemed to live by the maxim eat, drink and be merry for tomorrow we die. He was a thoroughly modern man. **" Lets Party!"**

As time goes on Isaac plans to pass on a blessing to his sons. Obviously this was a very important event.

There is a family plot to usurp Esau the oldest by a few minutes from the birthright due to the eldest. Jacob dresses up and fools the poor sighted Isaac that he is actually Esau.

Well we see these kinds of stories all the time don't we? Jacob gets found out, mother cries, Esau threatens to kill his wretched brother, and along come social services and take Jacob in. Well not quite, but certainly Jacob runs away and ends up sleeping rough.

On the journey back to the homeland of his father Isaac and grandfather Abraham he, along with many of similar generations, makes a spiritual journey too. He comes, so he tells us, into contact with the living God.

That doesn't seem to immediately change his rather self-centred character. However, it does make him God-aware.

Eventually he marries his sweetheart. Not before being at the receiving end of a few twists that are detrimental to him.

Maybe there is that 'what you sow you reap' factor in there somewhere. Jacob moves on, and later has that same God experience. Only this time it is not so ethereally sweet.

This time the meeting is much more real and much more painful. This time one can see character change.

It gives him an understanding of who he is, where he should be going, what he should be doing, and who and where he can get the power.

So much so that he even changes his name. No longer Jacob but Israel, Father of Nations. Isn't it so often the case that the fights, the struggles, the pain can produce what the nice sweet expectations failed to?

JACOB

Is it true that our current culture wants
things now?

Wants them instantly and want them *'to
make me happy'* usually without pain or
pressure or difficulty or battle or strife.
But really knowing about things and
having things of value isn't that cheap!

Jacob ends up with a big family, and as
is usual in families repeats some of his
father's and mother's and his
grandparent's problems, even to the
point of engendering that same family
pressure of squabbles and favouritism
that caused his children pain.

He also lived in that multi-sexual
experience that increases the confusions
and the rivalries and the tensions,
almost leading to murder.

Fortunately for Jacob, with the
protection of and Foreword planning by
his God, he ends up in old age
surrounded and cared for by his family.
The story ends well.

We
knew you as the
Superman. The
Hero to us all,
you were the
Superman

You
were the
Superman, the
hero for your
many sons. You
were the Superman,
the hero of Israel. With
super powers that
we all adored. That
when school friends
saw you, they
adored you,
spoke highly of the
man that belonged to
the sky. You were the superman, that took the next step of
Abraham, with presence that we fear,
Your words that were spoken, were jot-
ted down by us all, You were the Superman
and with your poor sight, you did not

man,
the tower of
strength
that solved
the petty pol-
itics that plagued
our spiritual lives.
Your voice sweeped in,
and your powers with-
in, swiped the
squarrels clean. You were
the Superman, who
strolled the Israel
Hood, Angels were
shuddered by your wis-
dom, as you spoke to your
disciples. Spending evenings in
the tavern, detailing the beautiful
attributes of your lover the Creator.
You were the Superman, that I couldn't
quite reach.

see your
m a n y
admirers
staring at
all your
glory as
your face
shined
t h e
beauty
of your
ancestors. You
were the Super

You were
t h e
Superman.
You were
the Super
man. You
were the
superman I
wanted to
know the Clark
Kent. You were the
S u p e r m a n

CHAPTER TWO

A FATHERLESS GENERATION

Less than one hundred years ago in the UK families were 'extended families'. People did move, but not on the scale that they do today. In the USA I understand that most people will move at least every two years. Probably not quite that bad in the UK but I reckon we are getting there.

A FATHERLESS GENERATION

Urban conurbations in the west often have large 'bed sit land', multiple occupancy buildings where much of the population will be transient.
In that kind of environment, relationships become short term, and tragically get thrown away along with the old Styrofoam cup from the take-away.

That tremendous change has taken less than one hundred years to activate.

Even sixty years ago in most areas you would, if you had lived in the UK, have been very close to much of your birth family.

Aunts and uncles, grandfathers and grandmothers, cousins and second cousins, all in constant contact and usually easily reachable; that environment created a further extension of the family with adopted aunts and uncles, and *'not really'* brothers and sisters who nevertheless belonged.

JACOB

All of that meant that there was a huge support network well-known to each other and the wider community, that could be expected to support in times of pressure and crisis.

I'm not saying that families then had no problems, or that extended family is the perfect model.

If you think that then just talk to someone from a current African extended family and listen to his or her problems. Some though work incredibly well.

Importantly what you do get in a closely interrelated community, in constant touch with wider family, is a modelling of parenting, mothers and fathers to look at, and at close hand.

With this wide choice of people who you might try and copy, hopefully you could just end up trying to be like the better ones. This wider view allows you to see more and hopefully chose better.

A FATHERLESS GENERATION

So if your parents where nasty or nutters, you could at least look at your cousin, or 'not really' brothers or sisters family and maybe theirs was more 'normal'. Usually you would be in close touch with several such families.

So your learning experience of what mothering or fathering entailed was broad.

However in the 60's and 70's we began to replace that extended family with what is nowadays perceived as 'normal family' which usually means dad, mom, 2.4 kids, mortgage and it used to be Metro, (I'm not sure what the current 2.4 family is running).

That became the 'norm'. In the 80's and 90's we moved on from there to a point where we are seeing increasing micro families, i.e. more usually it is mom and a child. Less often, but its there, dad and child.

Currently we are in a housing needs crisis.

JACOB

Not enough housing to go around. Now sure some of that is exacerbated if you live in the south, because it's supposedly good for work.

However the real pressure for housing is coming from the need to accommodate smaller and smaller families, and from the constant and exacerbated breakdown of even the dad/mom and 2.4 kind of family. If you get a divorce, even if there are only three of you, you need at least two sets of housing.

In some ways you can understand the dilemma of the modern generation. We have this silly assumption that you don't need to learn about relationships, marriage, fathering, mothering; we assume that those things come naturally.

They came naturally to our parents or grandparents, so they will to us.

A FATHERLESS GENERATION

That of course forgets that a great deal of learning is absorbed by the modelling of others, and that we learn a lot from watching and also from what our life experiences have taught us.

So if the pool we learnt from was so small, just our own nasty father say, or even nutty father, or most often '***the not there father***', how much do we know about how to father?

I am emphasising fathers, for although I realise that there are motherless children, it is more often that it is a man that is missing.

Surely this must be the most fatherless generation there has been.
In the west men are in a crisis of identity. There is a real reluctance on the part of men to take responsibility.

Men want contracts of relationships where it is not too difficult to opt out, and to take the responsibility of children? Oh please no!

In other countries we have a huge fatherless situation created by war.

JACOB

In still other countries there is a parentless epidemic created by Aids. It all leads to probably the largest ever parent disconnected generation, worldwide.

Now I'm sure there will be those reading this that say, "well my family was ok". Great, but the statistics should tell you that there is a serious breakdown out there. I think many women say, "I don't want to be tied into marriage" but they say it because they intrinsically know that men have already opted out of real commitment.

In preparing some people for marriage, I come across many 'modern' youngsters who say, "a piece of paper doesn't make a marriage, nor is it an indication of love". Of course that's true! However I'm very suspicious of those who don't want the piece of paper, because I think it's not the piece of paper that they don't want, but something more serious.

A FATHERLESS GENERATION

What they don't want is the risk of long term commitment, long term responsibilities the difficult of working through the bad times as well as the good. That's what is not wanted, **and that is a serious devaluation of love!**

The reason that we don't want that commitment is that we are not sure how to do it and we are not sure how to do it because we haven't seen it done, or modelled to us. Our life experience says it doesn't work.

But it does work. As part of a church community, I see it work, lots of times, not without problems, or bad times, but working through those times. One of my pleas for the church is to get involved with modelling really good family. Extend your family, draw in others, become a father not just to your own birth children but to the wider community. The world we live in desperately needs families.

Some of these problems must have existed in the early church age, for Paul the Apostle writes to the churches and says you are not short of teachers and preachers, but you haven't got many like me I'm your father.

This world needs fathers. Can you be one for your current generation?

There's a challenge, of course, if you're going to be one. Better learn how to do it well and right and good, so that you can pass on the skill!

Be counter culture. Be a committed man. Model fathering!

JACOB

CHAPTER THREE

HISTORY THAT PRODUCED US

We often don't take enough notice of cause and effect. We like what we see, we like what we taste. Why do we like what we taste? Probably because we were conditioned as youngsters, to eat the food of our parentage. If we had been born somewhere else, we would like other foods. Some of us have grown daring, it's true and are experimenters. But there are still many that know that what they eat and taste, how they live, and work and arrange things is the right way.

HISTORY THAT PRODUCED US

Never any thought is given to what made it right.

The things that mould us are both recent and ancient.

The Romans, of course, were world conquerors and along with their world conquest they brought not only the language and ways of doing things, but were great admiration of Greek culture.

That culture has invaded every area of modern history and it has produced us. Yes, and we need to know, ask the question, as we should of all cultural expression, 'is it right'? Not just simply is it right for me, but is it right? To ask is it right in the general sense you do of course need a standard against which to judge right and wrong, and that standard should be stable – do you have one?

Think about the things that are in our thinking and language that we can directly trace back to the Greeks. Think about the question of whether that is a right base line? Look at some of these Greek ways of looking at things.

Now, of course, we may have modernized it a bit, but look at the root of what the Greeks were saying. Can you see your picture in Greek mirror, and isn't the way that they thought and acted much the same as the ways that you think and act and presume is normality Today?

When you have looked in the Greek mirror then check out the Hebraic world view on the right!

A GREEK WORLD VIEW.

1. Mother earth is the impersonal source of all life on the planet.

2. Nature is a self-generating force, operating according to its own closed system of laws and acting independently of any authority outside of itself.

3. Nature is God and God is Nature. All that is, is natural. The supernatural simply does not exist. (Ionian thought)

4. The Olympian gods are personal yet limited, while nature is unlimited yet impersonal.

5. Man is classified as an animal, distinguished by this specific difference: man is a rational animal. (Aristotle)

HEBRAIC WORLDVIEW IN CONTRAST.

1. Father God is the personal source of all life on planet earth as well as the planet itself and all things beyond.

2. Creation is generated by the Creator God who made it for His purpose operating according to laws designed and sustained by Him and subject to His authority. While the Greek sees laws of Nature, the Hebrew sees laws over Nature.

3. Creation is God's handiwork. God is not to be confused with what he has made, for He existed prior to and is distinct from that which He created. He is a supernatural being, inhabiting the supernatural as well as the natural, created world.

4. The God of Abraham, Isaac and Jacob is unlimited yet personal.

5. Man is differentiated from animals and unique from all other living things in that he is the only creature made in the likeness of God.

GREEK.

6. Man's appearance on earth is the result of an impersonal, non-rational act of a force called Nature[1]. No purpose is involved. No meaning for existence is given. Mother nature is silent.

7. Man's value and worth is determined by the society into which he is born.

8. Truth is measured by man's intellect and reasoned judgement. There is no divine standard or measure of truth, which stands over and above man's determination. Man is the measure of all things.

9. The faith of Greek philosophers is built upon reason acting independently of divine revelation.

10. Religious expression is centred on rituals such as food offerings to gods and other rites. Correct ritual receives more emphasis than conduct. The gods do not speak to such issues as business, law, relationships, labour or family.

11. Religion is a personal choice, a private matter. There are many gods to worship and creeds to choose in Athens.

12. Moral conduct is relative to public opinion and / or individual conscience. The Greeks had no Bible to regulate thought and conduct. Values are relative to the social environment.

13. For the citizen of Athens, to show himself the rightful lord and owner of his own person in the entire manifold aspect of life is an exalted right. (Pedicles)

14. Human Freedom is self-determined.

HEBRAIC.

6. Man's appearance on earth is premeditated by a personal, rational Being and is a deliberate and decisive act of intelligence with purpose.

7. Man has intrinsic value because he is created in the image and likeness of God. He has God-determined worth, independent of society's opinion.

8. God determines truth, independently of man. Gods Word is the measure of all things. Mans opinion does not affect it in any way.

9. The faith of the Hebrews is built upon revelation from God, to which human reason submits.

10. Religious expression is a commitment to a way of life. God is as relevant to behaviour on the Sabbath as he is to what is done during the rest of the week. His word speaks to all spheres of life, be it business, law, relationships, labour or family.

11. God and His word are not dependent upon human acceptance or rejection. His reality and man's accountability to this reality stand, regardless of human consent.

12. Moral conduct is relative only to God's word and in that respect is absolute. Public opinion and individual conscience have no power to alter what God has declared true or morally right.

13. For the Hebrew, to show himself the rightful and obedient servant of GOD his maker and owner is his joyful blessing, a privilege and obligation.

14. Human freedom is God determined.

GREEK.

15. Wisdom is found from within.

16. Know thyself. (Socrates)

17. The Greeks learned in order to
                           comprehend.

18. The Greeks asked: "Why must I do it?"

19. In Sparta education is for the
obliteration of the individual in the service
of the state. In Athens, it is for the
training of the individual in the service
of culture.

20. Education is considered as the imparting of
knowledge from one person to another,
mouth to ear.

21. Philosophers view manual labour
as vulgar and beneath a citizens dignity.

22. Old age is feared.

23. History is viewed as a cycle of aimless
repetition. The same basic pattern of life
and death goes on with no particular end or
destination in sight.

24. The gods are created in the image and
likeness of man.

25. Man has no mandate from any
source above man himself.

HEBRAIC.

15. Wisdom is found from without. Foolishness is found within.

16. Know God.

17. The Hebrews learned in order to revere. (Abraham Heschel)

18. The Hebrew asked, "What must I do?" (Abraham Heschel)

19. In Israel, education is for the training of the individual in the service of God. (William Barclay)

20. Education is seen as the imparting of life; passing all you are to one another, mentoring.

21. Trades are honoured and manual labour is respected so much that Rabbis are expected to be proficient in a trade as well as the law.

22. Old age is honoured.

23. History is viewed as going somewhere, like an arrow to its target. Theirs is a straight-line concept of history with God working His purposes in the earth, culminating in the messianic reign of Israel's Redeemer.

24. Man is created in the image and likeness of God.

25.Man's divine mandate is to care for creation and to rule responsibly over the earth.

HISTORY THAT PRODUCED US

So on the other hand you have an
entirely different world view expressed
by what I call the Hebraic view. Look
at some of these Judaistic philosophies.
Isn't there a difference? Compare them
and then ask the question what would
be a right base line for life, what would
give a solid meta-narrative? Isn't it
necessary for me to have one if I am to
create change in my world? **Do I want
to create change, and can I see any
injustice?**

Coming more up to date we cannot
ignore the pressures that have been put
on our world in the last one hundred
years or so. Look at the immense
changes that have taken place, some of
them for good some of them not so
good perhaps. See my quick chart of
the decades, courtesy of the PEPA arts
company.

A SHORTHAND LOOK AT THE LAST DECADES.

40's War.
50's Expectation and hope
60's Freedom coupled with rebellion, the last modern teens.
70's Disillusionment, disappointment and frustration.
80's Materialism and look after number one.
90's Despair increase. In most sections of society, suicide also up. (New Musical Express survey).
00's????

We are going to look in the next chapter at our current culture. However let us just look at some of the major changes that have gone on through the above decades, all of which put us under pressure. Of course there are always changes going on in our cultures, however the fast rate of change that we have experienced over the last 7 or so decades is different to previous decades and for that reason presents us with particular pressures.

THE MAJOR CHANGES THAT HAVE AFFECTED OUR CULTURE.

- The Industrial Revolution
- The advent and pace of urbanisation
- The last world war (particularly the way it changed the nature and role of women)
- The **rate** of change within the world and particularly our culture
- The loss of absolutes
- The loss of a moral base
- The questioning of traditions (some questioning of which is most positive)
- The change taking place in many old institutions.
- The advance of technology
- The 60's, 70's, 80's, 90's collective cultural consciousness
- The loss of spirituality (which is being regained within post modern society (see next chapter)
- The increase in materialism
- The past belief / faith in science (which currently is being eroded).

CHAPTER FOUR

OUR CURRENT POST-MODERN WORLD VIEW

I am 57 years-old. When I left school, in the 60's in Birmingham, UK there were 12 jobs available for every 10 school leavers. Birmingham was dubbed the City of a thousand trades. I remember watching my first television programme, which was the coronation of the Queen in 1953. What a different world 2001 is.

Many of my age group will say things about the 'Jacob' generation like "I don't understand them, I don't know what makes them tick". Well that might be true, however their current culture is actual pervading all of us.

OUR CURRENT POST-MODERN WORLDVIEW

We might not understand but the changed world we now live in understand it or not, it is affecting us all.

The German Philosopher Tannwitz first used the phrase Post-modern in 1917. So the idea is not as new as some might think. The most famous formulation of post-modern philosophy was given by Gene Franswar Leotards in his 1979 publication, 'The post-modern condition', where Leotard defined post-modernity as an incredulity towards meta-narratives of which I will talk more about later; don't get frightened by the word. However the way we use the phrase post-modernism now has particular meaning.

Let's have a look at what I mean by post-modernism, and how that is affecting and shaping the culture today.

The world we live in is a world of images, information technology, mass advertising, sounds, smells, signs, and ways of doing things and acting which were unknown 50 years ago. Some were unknown 10 years ago.

JACOB

Even in 5 years huge changes have taken place. Look at a picture of a school playground even 5 years ago. What hits you is there is not a mobile phone in sight. Have a look at one today!

These tremendous changes have caused a massive shift in thinking and therefore in attitude and action, primarily started by the Jacobs, but spreading right through to the older generation (though we get there much slower).

The huge changes have caused massive challenges to old established institutions, be they political, economic, spiritual, educational and, most profoundly, that influencer that affects us probably the most powerfully, the media. This generation is a media generation.

It reacts in a way that no other has to images, art, and information overload. Watch that screen. Most TV programmes change the picture every three seconds. It's slow if you can count five.

OUR CURRENT POST-MODERN WORLD VIEW

All of these things have brought about huge change in the culture; here is a little chart for you of what I consider to be the positives and negatives of our current culture.

POSITIVES

- It loves stories.

- It desires a spiritual setting.

- It sees that materialism isn't
                    everything.

- It believes in justice.

- It respects the individual.

- It appreciates the present.

NEGATIVES.

- The stories are often disconnected.

- The spirituality is often pick and mix.

- The opposition to materialism it is
  often not thought through.

- Their justice has no *absolutes.*

- They don't realize individualism is not
  the sum total.

- The past is disconnected historically.

OUR CURRENT POST-MODERN WORLD VIEW

The stories that this generation so loves are often depicted in short sharp images. What is frustrating to an older generation is that they are not interested in how the stories connect to history.

There is the approach that what is happening now is the most important experience and even if the next experience contradicts the last it doesn't matter; what matters is the moment.

Fun as this is, we are foolish if we do not recognise that a long, long history has modelled us and made us.

The crux of the approach is the fact that the current culture does not have a Meta-narrative. I told you I would come back to that phrase. Meta-narrative means the big story, or big picture. Most of my age be they Jewish, Islamic, Christian, or Communist had a Meta-narrative. We believed in the big picture. There was a beginning and an end and we were somewhere in the middle. What you did could have value and a modelling influence, not just for yourself but also for others, and for even the future after you are dead.

JACOB

Not so current culture; it is the moment that counts.

The truth is I am saying that there are both positives and negatives of the current culture / generation. I think that we need to appreciate the positive and maybe the older generation needs to challenge the negatives.

For example it's great from my point of view that the new generation actually does not believe that materialism is everything and that they have a search for the spiritual. But on a negative side you can't, in my opinion have justice without a moral base or big story or lawgiver i.e. God.

Care for the individual is great, but we mustn't make that such a selfish action that we ignore responsibility for the wider community and the future.

In other words there is a big picture, there is a Meta-narrative and we need to persuade this generation that much of their agenda is good.

OUR CURRENT POST-MODERN WORLD VIEW

Their means of communication may be revolutionary to us, (my generation) but if what they do works and are understood that's great too.

Some of their values are well worth having, and some of their challenges to what my generation thought were right and valuable are well on time.

However there is a big picture and we can change the future, we can make a difference.

I would want to do it together: Abraham, Isaac and Jacob. But it's Jacobs shout.

Re Footnote:

All through this book *I make the assumption* that we arrive at conclusions in life, based on our presuppositions and assumptions. (Even though I don't always use the words Presupposition or Assumption). I believe that although we don't think about it, life actions are in fact based on these two things and they vitally affect our decisions. Hence this explanation footnotes.

Footnote:

PRESUPPOSITIONS AND ASSUMPTIONS

All of us, even though we say we don't, have a set of
presuppositions and *assumptions,* usually subconsciously
and usually never checked out. These *presuppositions* often
colour the 'factual' answers that we arrive at on life's
journey. The starting point of what we look at already has an
integral meaning which, although we don't like to think it, is
directly coloured by our *assumptions* (unspoken /sometimes
unknown at a verbal level). Being objective is much harder
than we think.

Dr. Christian Overman M.Ed. says:"It would be helpful to
most of us if we took a torch and examined the foundations
of our culture, and tried to understand our *assumptions* and
presuppositions." I *am thankful to Dr Overman's writings
for highlighting the differences in Greek and Hebrew culture,
and the effect that the Greek culture has had on most of the
western world, if not the whole world.*

51

CHAPTER FIVE

A JACOB CHURCH FOR THE 21ST CENTURY

Or a Jacob 's' church. What would it be like? Because the post-modern culture is modelling our current younger generation, not only are they questioning the old established institutions, including the religious ones but they are also questioning the received wisdom that science will solve all our problems.

In fact they are incredibly sceptical in that regard, maybe rightly so.

A JACOB CHURCH FOR THE 21ST CENTURY

Along with that scepticism of science there are searching desires to 'touch', beyond that which is just the material physical world. They are yearning after some kind of spirituality that gives meaning.

The problem with that search, and because of the 'let's live for the now experience, that's what's relevant' approach, there is a willingness to almost kiss all rational analysis goodbye. So we throw out cause and in effect we are almost back to Topsy in Uncle Toms Cabin: "I just growed." And of course we did not just grow or get here from nowhere.

We got here by a route and the journey has had a moulding effect on our belief system, which is conditioned by our presuppositions.

It isn't a blank sheet. This modern generation does need to consider what has brought us here.

JACOB

We do need to ask questions like "if I adopt this belief system, philosophy, way of thinking, how does it affect my actions and the way I treat others and the world I live in"?

We sometime, have this crazy idea that what we think has no affect on how we, or others act. Nonsense. Our belief systems and thoughts are irrevocably connected, both personally and collectively. Religious and or spiritual belief systems will produce a certain kind of world, nation or community.

A JACOB CHURCH FOR THE 21ST CENTURY

On one hand I applaud the post-modern desire for spirituality and meaning, and rejoice in the current generations healthy scepticism towards politician's scientist or any other ' ist' or so called specialists who presume to have got everything sussed for the rest of us, mere mortals.

Nevertheless we need some 'modernism' if that's what it is, of rational thought that asks questions as to, is this right spirituality? I deplore the idea that "its all right if it suits you" approach. Not to put to strong a point on it its just plain daft! It matters! It's a bit like two bottles of liquid in a cupboard, one is plain clear water, and one is deadly poison.

It does matter which you drink. It doesn't matter how sincere you are that they are both harmless, or that you spiritually choose to believe the best in both, I need a stronger word than daft for that approach *******!

So what kind of church for the Jacobs?

JACOB

In asking that we ask what kind of
church have we got anyway? Well to
use shorthand, it is usually building
focused, defiantly meeting focused; it
does tend to be inclusive if you are in
and irrelevant if you are out.

It is often hierarchical, male and bound
up in its own needs and practice.
Spending a lot of money on maintaining
itself, and looking after those who are
its members.

I guess we should then ask is that what
was intended for the church, is that how
it started and is that the best for now. I
think the answer to all of those
questions is no, no and no again.

It's obvious historically that the early
church didn't have any buildings,
probably before Constantine. It's
obvious to that although the early
church certainly met together, regularly,
probably daily, that meeting time was
much more of an eating together and
being together, supporting each other,
liking and loving each other, caring for
each other.

A JACOB CHURCH FOR THE 21ST CENTURY

Bearing each other's burdens, sharing each other's joys and sorrows, community in reality, not meeting without meaning.

It seems pretty obvious to me too, that church was a much more 'out there thing'. You got on with your job as a soldier, slave, servant or whatever. You were church wherever you where, wherever you found yourself and being church was defined by your active belief being demonstrated by actions.

Your relationships were to those who where Christ's followers or 'little Christs'. The important fact was, who was Lord? Not Caesar or self but Jesus.

It seems too, that church like this existed in the UK in Celtic times, before the imposition of Roman ways. A church that was flexible and spiritual but also outward looking, engaging with the real world and relevant to that world; an irritant very often perhaps, but isn't that just what we need now.

JACOB

A church that flows out of a committed Christ community, engaged in every area of the real world: business, politics, education, media, art, drama, theatre, etc., etc., Playing a very real *SALTING* role in the community. Salting in terms of bringing a challenge to unrighteousness, disharmony, dishonesty, destructive practice, dehumanising approaches to people and disempowerment of any section of humanity.

It should also be a church that models new inventions, new experiments, and new ways of doing things.
The trend-setter *LIGHT* in a world that needs to see Church at work.

Honest business enterprises that make profits to create more jobs, giving dignity to workers and operating honestly empowering people.

Immersing itself in meaningful art and theatre and media and the like, that shouts "here is the way!"
Making space for, influencing (salt) and modelling (light) every kind of legitimate human activity.

A JACOB CHURCH FOR THE 21ST CENTURY

Seeking The Kingdom, bringing it into our time space world. Can Jacob produce this Kind of church for this millennium, **I think its what's needed, don't you?**

CHAPTER SIX

BUT YOU DO IT WRONG

Around the circle that I move in over the last three or four years the question, "how should we do church?" has been posed over and over again, usually with no definitive answer. It may be that you have never asked that question, either because you have no interest in church, or because you have, and go and are sure that the way you experience it is obviously right.

For those who don't have any concept of 'church' I'm glad you are reading this book.

BUT YOU DO IT WRONG

Maybe I can capture you with something that, I am sure can be fantastic.

For those of you who know how church should be, well I have a lot of questions for you, and I would like to strain your grey matter somewhat!

I have mentioned already in this book the subject of cause and effect, and the fact that many people, particularly post-modern people, don't seem to connect the two. So what we have is things like "I hate cancer, but I love smoking". It seems we are able to disconnect the one from the other. We almost tell ourselves there is no cause and effect.

We do it in so many areas of life that perhaps it shouldn't surprise me that people constantly do it when it comes to church. The book of Proverbs has an interesting thought.

JACOB

It says in chapter 23 verse 7 that what is in the heart / mind comes out and produces what we are or will become. Put another way our belief system produces action. That original cause has an effect.

Now, because I do not believe that we have had 'church' right over the years I have wanted, where allowed to experiment, to think through and to ask awkward questions re this phenomenon called church.

If of course, you are one of those who has a set view that church is on the corner, a building that looks like so and when you go there it will have an hour or two of this and that and you know exactly what to expect. Then you will maybe have a problem with my question what is 'REALLY CHURCH'?

Church is a very predictable institution you may think. Some would say that's very true of the Anglicans.

BUT YOU DO IT WRONG

In reality it is also true of the Pentecostal, and the House churches. They have very predictable soft rock bands and the format does not change that much.

Of course I would applaud all experimentation that takes place in whatever church, but let's be honest, after a while the format takes over and people go through the process of the tried and expected happening and that can ultimately be very boring.

(Yet if it is what we know to do, we somehow feel guilty if we don't do it.) We usually don't ask "what is the purpose?" We very rarely ask "is this **REALLY CHURCH?"**

Now in North London, in the church of which I am part, the experiment is moving on apace. It is trying, and I would say often succeeding, to **BE** church rather than to **GO** to church. It is interesting. It is producing a very new, (or is it the old and original,) model?

JACOB

Church has become a multifaceted collection of small communities.

Often times sharing homes, definitely sharing meals, caring for one another, answerable to one another. Often caring in that Oh-so- difficult area of finance.

Yes from time to time there are gatherings together where those smaller communities can meet up with a larger collection of smaller communities.

There is structure and organization and there are many collective projects that the church participates in, for example running its own day school and nursery. However 'meetings' or that worse phrase 'services' are not church. They are what the church goes to, or does from time to time as appropriate.

In fact as I look around the group who lead this community of church I realize that each one of them is also a foster carer in the local community. Not that anyone has said you must be one; it is simply the out-working of real church.

I note too, that they are involved in the community in other ways, neighbourhood watch, assisting in schools encouraging local talent and the like.

From time to time people, usually those who have moved into the area and are looking for a 'church,' come along to one or other of the 'happenings'. Very often they make friends, (within our church community) sometimes they are helped with one issue or another.

However there are those who, whilst their body of friends, the people they would look to for help, the people who they would turn to if they are in need are this body of people, this church community

Church is 'being', and is being every day.

Not that the church is exclusive to its own. That would not be true at all.

Yet; nevertheless they know that when it comes to church we have got it wrong.

For that reason (because we have got it wrong) they go to 'The church with great preachers' some weeks, 'The church with teachers incorporated' others and 'The church with the really marvellous praise and worship group' when they really need a *'blessing'*.

Why have we got it so wrong?

Why are people so sure that the other way of doing church is right? Why isn't 'being' better than 'going'? My only answer comes back to cause and effect. The cause is our cultural expectations. We are a consumer culture.

BUT YOU DO IT WRONG

If you have been around church for a long time you know that what people want is: - To be fed (whatever that means) to be blessed, (and most have no idea what that means), and the feel good factor and that can be very subjective.

To be really rude they are looking for consumer feelings. They want to be able to say, "I am being entertained here". "I like this. I understand it".

We sample preachers, music, happenings, Bible study, teaching, tingle experiences, and get our kicks out of them in the same way as others would get satisfaction from the theatre, a good film, a football match, shopping, cuckoo clocks or whatever.

We are consumers. The materialistic society puts our feel good factor / need at the centre and so we expect 'church' to give us the same experience.

We want it to take care of us, coddle us, meet our needs, make us feel good, bless us, and everything else, because we are the centre of the universe.

If 'consumer church' does not do that then "oh well we can go to D, E, or F church as they may have a better show".

Statistics in the UK show that this is actually what is happening.

Going back to that cause and effect, the very people who use such churches, and I think use is the right word there, these people come back, when in trouble, to the North London lot for help!

It's not that I think that the people in traditional churches wouldn't try to help, that would not be true. Often there are good people there, and good management leadership.

I suppose my question would be a more fundamental one. Is it really church, or is it something else?

BUT YOU DO IT WRONG

The problem is that the system they are in mitigates against being what I would call real church.

When they have real need they come back to the *'wrong church'* because that's where their real friends are. These people will really try to help, these people have got something. We like these people.   That's what they say. The only problem they say is that (we) just
" Don't know how to run church"!

CHAPTER SEVEN

CURRENT CULTURAL PROBLEMS

I would like to take a little more time to look at some of the problems that post-modernism presents to us, coupled with some of the things that our current generation has thrown at us which need further examination; a definitive critical look or analysis. For starters, if you go to schools and talk to this generation about things like justice, they are angry about many injustices, and rightly so.

However being angry doesn't ultimately cut it. You have got to do something to change things.

The problem in the UK is that many of this generation have, it seems to me, been conditioned to believe that there are great problems out there but they are just 'one' and can't change anything.

I am here to say that's rubbish. Just a *one* can make a real difference, **(It only takes one.)**

Then there are the ***STORIES THAT ARE DISCONNECTED.*** This generation loves stories. They are into them. They are great storytellers. But history is also important. A recent survey in the UK papers found that knowledge of history in UK schools has fallen to such a level that many children believe Hitler was the wartime leader of the UK. There were many other frightening gaffs.

History produced us. We need to know and understand the events that have made and modelled us, be those religious or political. We need to know about the warriors that fought for freedom of women and slaves. We need to know about economics and people who have changed the way we can live.

What were their persuading beliefs?
What was their motivating power?
Find that and maybe we can take the
future.

Believe that it is only the moment that
counts and we have understood nothing.

After that comes *PICK AND MIX
SPIRITUALITY.* The UK Daily Mail
recently ran a large article on what was
wrong with the Church in Britain.
The ultimate conclusion of the article
was that what we need is a church that
operates on a pick and mix spirituality
basis. That really would blow it.

What was advocated was that
Christianity should adopt all the nice
bits of different religions. Bits of
Hinduism, bits of Islam, bits of this, bits
of that. But just the nice bits of course.
Choose what people like; that's what
they do in the stores isn't it?
Consumerism again.

Of course what they were concerned
about was filling 'church' up (church
buildings for services and meetings that
is).

Whilst it's true that we can see facts from different angles, and it's true that we are on a journey in terms of knowing God, nevertheless you don't get to Dover in the south of England by heading North on the M1 to Manchester. Jesus did of course say **He** was the door! Again we miss out that cause and effect; effect!

Culture is a changing process and you don't get experimentation by maintaining an approach that says, "we have always done it this way and long may it continue" attitude. That way makes it impossible to be a pioneer. We need change and development, we need to look at things from a different perspective, we defiantly need to be asking questions and sometime we need to be sceptical of what is and has been done.

Yes, this new generation is somewhat *SCEPTICAL OF MATERIALISM.* That's a healthy thing I would agree. But are they sceptical enough?
It is quite hard on the one hand to decry capitalism and materialism whilst we are enjoying its fruits.

JACOB

A recent survey in a South London Youth Group, after lectures on majority world issues, after learning that around a billion people live on less than a dollar a day, the group was invited to list the things that they could manage life without. It was a good list. Then they were asked to list what they couldn't manage without.

We found strangely that these 14 to 17 year olds found it totally unthinkable that they could manage without their designer trainers, non materialistic as they were claming to be. I wonder how typical that is.

Many middle class people who go on about 'wishing to identify with the poor' also bemuse me; they want to give away their TVs and the like. I'm sure the poor would be saying, that's great, give them to me. The poor don't want to be identified with particularly, they would much rather be rich!

JUSTICE is the cry, but *POST-MODERN THINKERS HAVE NO ABSOULUTES*.

If you don't have a Meta-narrative then you won't have absolutes. There is no beginning. Where is the end? 'What happens now is important'. It is also strangely irrelevant if you don't have a start and a finale!

'If it feels good do it'. 'If you are sincere that's fine'. ' If that's what you believe that's great for you, I believe something else'. And so we could go on.

The problem is that if you don't have any absolutes, if you don't have a Meta-narrative then justice becomes an irrelevance. What do we mean by justice? For who? For why? If it's good for me and it hurts you then I cant let it stop me because I am the centre of my own world! I want MY freedom, I want what I want, I want it now, and I don't want any interference. Certainly I don't want any guilt or lawgiver. I would much rather you or someone else takes that responsibility.

Justice like that is no justice at all.

JACOB

No lawgiver, meaning no real reason
for law and no purpose to life or death,
care or justice. Cruelty is just the luck
of the draw, with no real meaning. **I
want a reason for being here and a
reason to fight for justice.**

The *INDIVIDUAL* and his / her
opinions is respected and appreciated.
That's so positive.
But it's not the sum total of what we
need. Yes I want to respect people's
freedom to disagree with me, but
freedom without responsibility is not
freedom. It is war. Yes I want to
acknowledge the rights of the
individual, but is that at the expense of
the community?

Recently I was shopping for some
office equipment. The shop owner, a
Muslim immigrant to the UK, launched
into a tirade against our culture. I'm not
sure what had made him mad, I only
know that I got the lot.

He fumed at me; "I want to be happy, that's all I hear people say in this country, I want a good time,
I want to go on holiday, I want to be rich, I want, I want, I want!!! Whatever happened to responsibility?" he said. "Life is not about being happy, it's about being"… I quickly paid my bill and beat a hasty retreat, as he was getting more wound up. **But I totally agree!**

So there are things in this current culture that we ought to want to change. If we are to affect our world we need to be change agents. If we really want to affect the things that matter we have to do things, we have to affect things. **And we can.**

We ourselves have to be working in the opposite spirit to some of the things in the culture; we have to be **counter culture!**

CHAPTER EIGHT

MODERN CULTURAL BENEFITS

Some cynics would say that there are no benefits to our modern world. I am not one of those. I think used correctly there are some tremendously helpful things in our current post-modern culture.

First is the *LOVE OF STORIES,* which encompasses a whole host of things. This generation is incredibly creative.

MODERN CULTURAL BENEFITS

It communicates in stories, but not just from the picture story. Even though I personally dislike soaps, they are nevertheless continually creative stories. So creative that some unfortunate people try to live like them.

Advertising, be it TV or posters or whatever is often story based.

Our modern creative society is adept at communicating with an infinite variety of visually stimulating images, and telling us the story, be it product or personal, in an infinite variety of ways.

Art is bursting at the seams. It pushes the edge of every boundary, be it in paint, sculpture, layout, animation, drama, installations, advertising, and on and on. It uses, and continually invents, new media, such as the Internet, wap phones, text messages, picture messages, blue tooth tec knowledge, and again on and on.

Sadly, those who claim to be in touch with the multi-facetted, painter of all painters, artist of all artists, communicator par excellent, creator God Himself, still tend to try to communicate to this diverse, created in the creator's image culture, in a bland boring two dimensional way. Black text on white paper, with some words thrown to people sitting in rows, usually called a church meeting. **The creator demands better than that!**

SPIRITUAL DESIRE is another plus for our modern culture.

Sure it searches in every wacky, daft area that there is, and tragically there are a million blind alleys compared to 'the way,' however it demonstrates some very **positive** things.

It's positive to recognise that science, so called, does not have the answer to every ill of man. **It's positive** to recognise that material success does not bring ultimate fulfilment and satisfaction to life.

It's positive to assume that there must be more to life than eighty or ninety years. **It's positive** to want to search out something that is beyond the obvious nose on your face. **It's positive** to desire some answers to the needs of justice in the world in which we live.

The challenge of that positive desire for a spiritual dimension is that we don't squander it on non sense.

To avoid doing that I would suggest three things: -

JACOB

1. *Check out what the spiritual path you are looking at has produced in others. Don't just take the easy option of a dreamy non critical 'oh its so nice approach'.*

2. *Look at what is being produced or in most cases not produced in real life, in real support for the marginalized and dispossessed of our world. In other words is there definable cause and effect?*

3. *Check out its historical lineages. Things don't come about by just appearing, except in fiction and where there is a profit to be made from the gullible.*

Another area, maybe a weak one but it's definitely there in our current culture, is that of **DOUBTS ABOUT MATERIALISM**.

MODERN CULTURAL BENEFITS

Sure it could be stronger, but we are seeing the frustration of the modern generation sometime expressed in things like riots in the USA and in the Czech republic over frustration at world money systems.

Oh I know the critics would argue that these people used materialistic air transports and travel etc. to get there but don't throw the baby out with the bath water. There is disillusionment growing there. Quite right too.

This current culture wants *JUSTICE.* I have already alluded to the weakness of a justice desire without a Meta-narrative or absolutes.

But at least if you desire something good you have taken the first steps on a very important journey. Maybe the journey, in time will show that you cannot have justice in a vacuum. Then you start looking for a meaning, and 'A WAY'.

INDIVIDUAL RESPECT is both a blessing and a curse. I believe that the God I serve loves and respects the individual. I actually believe He wants a relationship with the individual. What is awful though is to make the individual god. That is to some extent what our culture has tried to do. The cult of number one. How many advertisers tell us they are looking after number one. That's you.

Sure we need respect of individual liberties, freedom, rights to speak, to choose, rights to disagree, rights to life, rights, rights, rights!

YES, but it is totally untenable to think that we can have rights in isolation of responsibilities, and the balance of communities the group collective. That too must be in its rightful place. balancing those rights we think we should have.

IT ENJOYS AND APPRECIATES THE PRESENT. What a big plus that is.

MODERN CULTURAL BENEFITS

Too many of the 'modern generation' didn't. In the UK we still have a heritage of it.

Some in this country are still saying how good the past was or how much better it might be in the future, (not the post-modern culture) the antithesis of such enjoyment.

We believed that we could only enjoy when we got into the future, when we had got a degree, when we had got a decent career, when we had arrived at stability, when we had, fill in the missing word..... Always pushing our satisfaction to some future state.

Actually we were being robbed of the present.

JACOB

Then, when we got to that supposed
future state we constantly went on, and
still do, about the good old days, how
good they were, the summers were
warmer, the winters were prettier, the
children better, the teens more polite.
Hey I was there. It was not that good,
but yet again it was, and is, a robbery of
the now. The present is all that you
have, use it wisely, and enjoy.

**It is only from the present that we
have any possibility of changing the
future, and thus affecting history.**

JACOB

CHAPTER NINE

THINKING CHANGES EVERYTHING

Every action starts with a thought. Sure our bodies don't think about thinking in some instances. When you drive a car for a long time it's very different to when you first start. But all actions, what we do and what we are, start by thought.

Again, Proverbs 23 verse 7: what is inside our head will eventually come out in our actions.

THINKING CHANGES EVERYTHING

I guess that is why I really get angry with the ad men who want to claim that there is no detriment to our society by what it is they put on our small and large screens.

Then they pay vast sums of money to advertise on those same screens to persuade us to purchase their product, whilst all the time they know that paying good money for such advertising has no effect on us. Who are they kidding?

I get angry too with the modern youngster who tells me that it doesn't matter what they watch on television, what they read or what they hear, as if putting rubbish and dangerous materials into their brains was not going to have any effect. I get mad at such naivety, there needs to be a more thoughtful response.

I do like the computer people's phrase of 'GIGO' that I am led to believe means, in computer speak, garbage in garbage out. Which could equally apply to our thoughts!

JACOB

On the larger scale of things I want to say thanks to my friend Chris Bulpitt for the following guest chapter (as well as the Foreword to this book).

I think that what he is saying could affect our thinking on the macro scale as well as on our own individual lives.

I think you will find there is a lot to think about in Chris's Chapter. And to use Management speak, there is a lot to unpack. Some having seen Chris's paper, would say "oh yes I believe that." Then if you believe it, it will definitely change the way you act and of course that is the crunch point. **Action!**

Here is what he has to say....

GUEST CHAPTER
ETHOS

How can we be followers of Jesus as a community and live out the call to be salt and light with relevance and effectiveness? What ethos[1] do we need to embrace as a community of faith and what ethos would hinder us from being trail blazers and cutting edge people for Jesus and the Kingdom?

---

[1] Ethos can be described as the distinctive character, spirit and attitudes of a people group, community, culture or era. In the context of this paper it is akin to worldview or, as some have termed it, genetic code within the life of a church community.

ETHOS

I am proposing that there are two sets of ethos, and the aim of this chapter is to concentrate on this issue by contrasting these two sets, which I will call

Ethos 1 and Ethos 2. (Referred to from now on as E1 and E2).

I am further proposing that, whether we consciously embrace the issue of ethos or not, we all have an ethos. Even the attitude that says there is no such thing as ethos is an ethos in itself! My argument is that evangelical, charismatic church cultures are either E1 or E2 in leaning. There is a spectrum between E1 and E2, however, there is a pivotal point along the spectrum which determines whether a person or community leans toward E1 or E2. (I hope my diagram will illustrate it better than I can say it see next pages).

In my view most of the practical, personal and relational realities and tensions we can face throughout the wider 'evangelical/charismatic' church relate directly to this issue of ethos.

JACOB

Without apology I take an E2 position, which will become evident as I proceed.

I happen to believe that E2 is more true to the outworking of a Christocentric hermeneutic.[2]

I believe E2 is the attitude and culture that will enable us to enter further into the freedom we already have to be wild followers of Jesus who are flexible, asking questions and journeying on together to know Jesus and make Him known.

---

[2] This means that we approach the Bible and our faith in a distinctly Christ centered fashion. The entire Bible has to be interpreted through a Christ centered lens. For instance, this means our model for life is Jesus in the Gospels. The way that He operated shows us the way that we should live, do church, express leadership, interpret scripture etc.

For example, in terms of leadership, if we draw From Old Testament we need to see them in the light of Jesus' leadership.

There are huge implications to this approach.

ETHOS

Spectrum I have set out the main part of this paper in table form, which starkly contrasts the two sets of ethos. In reality there is a spectrum between E1 and E2. There is hard and soft E1 and soft and hard E2. The soft ends of each ethos are nearer the border line between E1 and E2 and hard ends are the extremes further away from the border line. In other words it looks similar to the political spectrum. The harder the ethos is the more extreme it is either as E1 or E2. The softer the ethos is the less extreme it is either as E1 or E2 as in the diagram below.

| HARD E1 | SOFT E1 | ▲ SOFT E2 | HARD E2 |

Stark Contrasts This contrasting table highlights the main distinctives of each ethos which could be further unpacked, which I might do one day but that would be a book in itself!

JACOB

By Box Experience (As shown in my first diagram following). I mean living in an environment in which belief and practice are very tight leaving very little space for questions and thus it is like living in a box.

In this kind of environment everything in the box is viewed as Biblical, right and true and everything outside of the box is viewed as being unbiblical, wrong and false. This leaves very little room for exploration and adventure either in thinking or practice.

In contrast to this is what I have called Base Experience, by which I mean an environment which is more like a base camp from which adventure, discovery and journey can be experienced as long as the base has Jesus at the centre, is strong relational community, has the scripture as a signpost pointing to Jesus and is open to the indwelling Spirit.

ETHOS

There is a lot of room and space to discover fresh theory and practice which will release lots of energy for advancing the Kingdom and experiencing church as a relational reality.

In my view these two forms of experience are the starting point of understanding E1 and E2.

ETHOS 1.

Heretical

Biblical
Orthodox   Unbiblical
Sound

Unsound

LEGAL BASE

Fixed view of church

GOD'S WILL is a tightrope

- Superstitious in outlook
- Can't make mistakes
- Orientated to the past – what has been

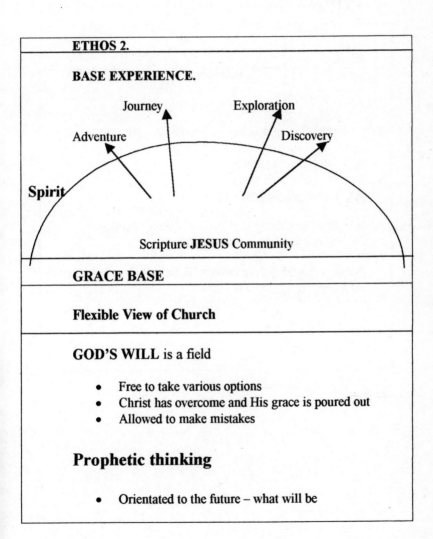

ETHOS 2.

BASE EXPERIENCE.

Journey   Exploration

Adventure   Discovery

Spirit

Scripture **JESUS** Community

GRACE BASE

Flexible View of Church

GOD'S WILL is a field

- Free to take various options
- Christ has overcome and His grace is poured out
- Allowed to make mistakes

Prophetic thinking

- Orientated to the future – what will be

ETHOS 1

BIBLE

BIBLE is approached in 'proof text' manner

- Text bound approach

- Law book, propositional

- Bible is Word of God in itself – often 'flat book' approach taken to interpretation

Bible is central with Jesus in the Bible and proof texts having authority. Irrespective of context.

ETHOS 2

BIBLE

BIBLE is approached in 'context' manner

- Christocentric approach

- Reference point, story

- Bible is inspired record pointing to the Word of God who is Christ

Jesus is central with Bible as a pointer to Him along with the Spirit and the community of faith

ETHOS 1

PROTESTANT/ROMAN MODEL of church

Church is –

Teaching centre of the Bible with a minister who teaches and people who listen and are 'built up' and 'fed' by hearing sermons. This teaching approach could be seen as pandering to people's wants from and E2 perspective.

TEACHING is through sermons from expert minister to inexpert congregation

- Greek style of teaching

Church tends to be seen as a sheepfold and sheep are to be fed and cared for by minister

LEADERSHIP is hierarchical and usually male because of approach to scripture i.e. text bound, proof texting

PROFILE/PLATFORM is favoured

- Profiling and platforming of 'superstars' is quite prominent

ETHOS 2

PNEUMATIC/CELTIC MODEL OF CHURCH

Church is –

A people who continue God's ongoing story in Acts by 'fleshing' it out. The Bible gives a point of reference for this ongoing 'fleshing' out of the story. This could be seen as being light on teaching from an E1 perspective.

TEACHING is more interactive, a participative community approach where none are experts and all are empowered

- Hebrew style of teaching

Church tends to be seen as a mission body into the wider community. The church is the corporate minister

LEADERSHIP is non-hierarchical and also female as well as male because of approach to scripture i.e. Christocentric, contextual.

SIGNIFICANCE/GRASSROOTS is favoured

- Everyone can be effective and superstar culture is seen to undermine the release of grassroots activity

ETHOS 1

DUALISTIC

- Sacred / secular divide. Things agreed with are called 'sacred'. Things disagreed with or frightened of are called 'secular'

- Leads to a tendency to withdraw from the world in fashion, music, literature. ideas

- Takes a defensive line towards the world because it's fallen and demonic

WORSHIP, which is seen as vital, is singing in a reflective manner to the Lord in meetings

"I meet with the Lord in meetings"

CULTURE is seen as irrelevant. All expression of church life is seen as merely normal and cultureless or, in some cases, as God's own culture

- From the perspective of E2 this usually amounts to a 'Christianising' of a narrow band of middle class culture

ETHOS 2

HOLISTIC

- No sacred / secular divide. The only secular thing is sin – everything else is welcomed

- Leads to a tendency to move into the world both to transform it and learn from it. Open to fashion, music, literature and ideas

- Takes an active Christocentric line towards the world because it's created by God and Christ is redeeming it.

WORSHIP is a whole lifestyle that includes singing. Singing, however, may not be worship. Lifestyle determines this

"My life is an ongoing meeting with God"

CULTURE is seen as vital and all expression of church life is seen as culturally relevant or irrelevant in relation to the wider community

- Any cultural expression is good and wholesome provided it is Christocentric, which, of course, always involves Jesus centred attitudes and values and has nothing to do with such cosmetic issues as fashion and cultural taste

ETHOS 1

DIFFERENT means wrong in most cases.

STATEMENTS AND ANSWERS to almost everything are valued highly. Things must be answered quickly

  • Questions tend to be dangerous

STRUCTURAL in approach to making thing happen.

HOLINESS is attained by pushing sin away.
E2 would see this as living a restrictive
lifestyle and often being legalistic in approach.

  • From an E1 perspective will often have an expression, which is 'heavy' on all sorts of issues. This expression would be seen by E2" as religious and legalistic.

CHURCH WILL BE A FOCUS and often there will be a tendency to concentrate on church structural issues. E2 would tend to see this as getting caught up on tenth-rate issues

ETHOS 2

DIFFERENT MEANS NOT NECESSARILY WRONG but usually a different perspective on an issue

QUESTIONS AND DISCUSSION are highly valued and lived with, without immediately trying to answer them

- Questions lead us on in the journey

RELATIONAL in approach to making things happen

HOLINESS is attained by passionate intimacy with Jesus, which causes sin to lose its strength

- Will often have an expression, which is 'light' on all sorts of issues. This expression would be seen by E1 as flippant, 'wishy washy' and 'airy fairy'

KINGDOM WILL TEND TO BE A FOCUS and all other issues would tend to be secondary to this kingdom mindset. E1 would tend to view this as threatening to church order and stability

ETHOS 1

CONSUMERISM of church tends to be strong. Consuming of Bible text sermons and singing would be high due to Protestant tradition of E1

- Protestant model tends to produce consumers.

A QUESTION OFTEN ASKED IS, 'What is my ministry?' A lot of emphasis put on individual calling and ministry

- Tendency to '**presidential**' style of leadership. One senior pastor with assistants leads the church. E2 would see this as one man (and usually a man!) dominated – paying lip service to a team

ETHOS 2

PRODUCTION would tend to be strong. Each church member produces and contributes although there is a 'force of gravity'. This tends to pull back into consumer mode because of the force of the protestant model

- Pneumatic model tends to produce producers.

A QUESTION OFTEN ASKED IS, 'where do I belong?' A lot of emphasis put on corporate calling and expression

- Tendency to **'prime ministerial'** style of leadership. Team leads the church with a team leader. E1 would see this as too team orientated with not enough emphasis on the number one leader (a term used in E1)

CONCLUSION

There are many others issues that I could highlight in order to help clarify this distinction between E1 and E2 but I think this would be unnecessary.

I think once you see the issue you can do your own thinking on all sorts of different areas.

The starting place of these two sets of ethos is the type of experience with which an individual or group begins. By definition, a commitment to box experience is always restrictive because the limits of the 'box' are the limits of the boxed person's world.

On the other hand, living from a base as explained previously, leads to adventure and journey. Jesus is the core of the base but it also includes an experience of real community, an openness to the Spirit and drawing from Scripture as our Story and reference point.

ETHOS

If any one of these three elements is missing from the base, E2 could lose its way. Charismatics have tended to emphasise the Spirit, but sometimes in very individualistic ways which have fed into the I me', 'mine' culture of the Western world.

I believe E2 is a strong enabling ethos and although it doesn't appear to have the numerical support and consensus that E1 has, I believe it is the future. I think it is at its best, profoundly Jesus centred and very enabling.

By saying all I've said in this chapter I <u>am not </u>saying E1 is completely wrong – anymore than I'm saying E2 is completely right. E1 is after all, within its own terms, very successful.

I **<u>am </u>** saying, however, there is another way of expressing church, which will engage many people in our society who have no hope and long for a vibrant, non-religious faith, which reveals Jesus in His glory and unconditional love.

CHAPTER TEN

ARE YOU BEING ROBBED?

Post-modern young people have a respect for the opinions of others. They often have a respect even for those who disagree with them. Yet in the area that I am about to talk about all that good stuff disappears in the morning mist!

The subject is sex. Are you being robbed in that area? At the end of the 20th century and the beginning of a new millennium, we live, at least in the west, in what is called sexual freedom.

ARE YOU BEING ROBBED?

Now if by freedom, we mean freedom in terms of   open understanding of our bodies, freedom in terms of education, freedom as to the right of people not to be abused, freedom from Victorian hypocrisy, then I'm all in favour of such freedom.

But the big question is do we abuse our freedom? Now I'm not talking about abuse of children, and I know that happens, and we are all anti that except those who do it. But I mean abuse of each other, male and female. And by that abuse we actually end up committing robbery of ourselves. We cannot look at our culture or our thinking without talking through this area.

Do we respect each other? I think not. Do we respect ourselves? Well actions suggest we don't or at least suggest we have been robbed or sold a lie.

JACOB

What do I mean? Well speaking now as an oldie, and watching and listening it seems we treat the opposite sex as an item, as a thing, as a personal recourse for us, either to be conquered or captured. Now if we used such language in any other area of life we would think that people were creating slavery, dehumanising people, at the very least being disrespectful. Aren't we?

If sex is simply a bodily function, drive to be satisfied wherever I can get it, it doesn't matter treating the other person like a thing or an object. Is that a good thing to do to another human being?

If sex needs lots of experience with lots of partners so that we are expert, what does that reduce the partners to that we had before the one we have got now. A thing?

Now through this book I have tried to be fairly non prescriptive. I know that you can think.

ARE YOU BEING ROBBED?

However I am about to depart from that approach for a moment, partly because I think that the media, the education system, and the nonsense of the 60's of which I was a part have done such a massive con job of selling unreality that I would like to lay out what **I think**. Then you can think it through even further, and live or not with the implications.

Over and again I have referred in this book to the fact that all actions start in thought. What you **think** about others and yourself starts there, and our innermost philosophies and presuppositions will present themselves in actions.

The actions that our thoughts produce will demonstrate themselves in actions that affect us and actions that have implications for others.

Now if **I think** that I am just an animal; then surely the way I treat others and myself will reflect that inner philosophy. So sex is just an animal function, and so I act that way towards others and myself. No surprise there.

JACOB

If **I think** the universe is simply mechanical ultimately **I think** of my actions as mechanical, I will tend to treat others, life, sex in a mechanical way.

If **I think** of the universe as an accident and I am part of that accident of nature, then of course who I have sex with and when and why and how is irrelevant. It's all an accident. Even the implications are accidental. It will be accidental for my partner, as well as for me.

If **I think** that life has no meaning, that nature put us here without meaning or purpose, then sex has no meaning or purpose. It just is.

If **I think** that there is no lawgiver, meta-narrative, moral universe, or ultimate justice then my sexual attitudes and actions will demonstrate that inner thought. Why should I act responsibly, to whom, for whom, and for why?

ARE YOU BEING ROBBED?

So it does not surprise me at all that we live in a world where this rather special, beautiful area of life causes so much pain and destruction. Please, please don't say that it does not. For that would be the biggest lie, and simply compound the robbery and the con.

So how do we effect change in such an important area. Well I will tell you what **I think** then maybe you can **think** some more.

I don't **think** we are just animals. We are something better and different to that. We are created in the image of the lawgiver and have a much greater understanding of such things as sex.

I don't **think** we live in simply a mechanical universe. **I think** that my actions are valuable and count. They make a real difference to me others and the future. They are important.

I don't **think** we are simply the result of nature. **I think** we are here by design, and have a brilliant designer at that.

JACOB

I don't **think** we are an accident, even
if our parents thought that! **I think** we
have a purpose to fulfil.

I don't **think** sex is dirty, prohibited,
embarrassing, not to be talked about,
not to be understood. **I think** our
sexuality is an incredibly important part
of life, of the Lawgiver's plan, and of
us.

I think that sex is much more than just
a physical act; I think it has
implications for both parties, not just at
the point in time when it takes place but
it stays with us for the future.

I think that all sexual intercourse
attaches us to people, not just
physically, but creates emotional 'soul'
ties that stay with us for life, even when
we are not aware of it, even when we
have submerged our feelings into our
subconscious thoughts, to the point
where we are not consciously aware.

ARE YOU BEING ROBBED?

I think that sex in a committed relationship draws a couple together, is fulfilling, is actually the designer's idea and improves and reaches better levels as time goes on.

I think that this current generation is being robbed, and spoiled in this area, and they are missing out on what is really good, settling for something that is of a much lower level, not top quality**, I think they are being robbed.**[3]

---

[3] LAW. I use the words law and lawgiver not in the sense of the Ten Commandments or the law of the land; but rather in the same way that what we refer to so called natural laws such as gravity, or aerodynamics. I don't like the word natural law. For me the same one, who designed moral law, is the lawgiver to the natural law.

JACOB

A little story of the forward girl beauty. Who came up to me and said 'Would you go to bed with me". Bloody hell I replied. how far down the list was I. Actually, don't answer that. TAXI TAXI TAXI TAXI TAXI. We enter the cab, She whispers kisses in my ear. The Fragrance of hair runs down to the nerves in my right leg and I kick the driver. DRIVER DRIVER, CAN'T YOU GO ANY FASTER. We step out the cab and I pass over a sweaty tenner. I see the curtains of neigboring windows shuddering from side to side. Hey neighbor, this is my lover. She's gonna go to bed with me, don't tell my mother. Hey neigbor, this is my lover. She's gonna go sleep with me, don't tell my f a t h e r .

We Enter, Sleep Together. She Wakes Up, Can't Remember, I Ask For Her Number, She Says Never, Then She Scarpers, I'm Kacked On By the Gift of the Creator. I Then Vomit. Vomit, Vomit.... But then, it's O.K. as I have discovered the truth, the truth that it was just a dream, it was a dream and I'm stil, yes still a virgin, I'm a virgin, I'm a sexy dic- in-tact virgin. I'm a sexy virgin. I LOVE VIRGINITY!

CHAPTER ELEVEN

HOW DO YOU EAT AN ELEPHANT?

And of course everyone answered, one bite at a time. Now don't knock it. If we are to change our culture, change the injustices in our world, change our thinking, then it will have to be one step at a time.

HOW DO YOU EAT AN ELEPHANT?

Or as *Dr Donald Howard, American Educator says: "We will have to have bite-sized achievable objectives".
That means we have to start the journey one with step.

About ten years ago my wife and I started to foster children. We did not do it because we had carefully thought it through, it sort of just happened.

We are glad that it did happen because it means we have met some great kids, some who are still well in touch and some who I still hope will be those who are counter culture for their generation.

We were just 'us', but as we did it we talked with others, then others fostered. I have already alluded to the fact that all of the Rainbow Church current leadership foster at the time of writing this book. I really did not anticipate that happening when we started. It did. It is the small beginnings that make a big difference.

---

*Founder of Accelerated Christian Education.

JACOB

If every one does a little bit a big bit gets done.

It seems to me that many of the new upcoming generation, say 13 up, have been or are being conditioned to believe that the problems of the world are so big what can you do.

Some feel so small they think they can do nothing, they feel they are just one against systems, injustice, and because the thing that needs changing seems so big what can just one person do? That feeling of inadequacy seems to be there amongst many. I want to shout to them start, do what you can, even if you perceive it to be oh so small, you will be surprised, **and you will make History.**

CHAPTER TWELVE

THE CURE (OR IS IT THE CHALLENGE?)

Why did I write this book? Partly to express the fact that there is a lot going for our current culture. At the risk of repeating myself the new generation is a one that is incredibly creative and expressive in a multiplicity of ways. In fact it's a great time to be alive.

As you will have gathered though I am troubled by the weakness of the culture and its inability to connect to the big picture. The robbery that it is facing.

I also have great faith in this new Jacob generation; I believe that they can do things.

Things like change the world in which they live for the better.

However to make a real change they are going to have to connect to real spirituality. Not the airy-fairy kind, but the living God kind.

They are going to have to get to know the lawmaker for themselves. Not second hand. Unlike us I don't believe that **Father** God has grandchildren, only beloved children.

I also believe that the **Father** wants personally to connect with this generation, as He does with all ages at all time. However to do that there has to be a searching and a finding. Not the kind of searching that is palmed off with 'if it feels nice, it must be all right.' Or the kind of nicely, nicely searching that dishonestly says: "As we are all searching any answer will do."

I choose to believe that this creative generation can grasp the fact that Father God has a plan. That God has a purpose, for them and the world.

JACOB

That God has a Kingdom that needs to be pursued, and that this Kingdom has a righteous just King that they can play an important role in bringing back to this planet.

When 'the spirit and the bride church say come' (of which body we can be a part) He the King will come, and with Him will bring the righteousness and justice that in the hearts of this generation very many want.

I believe that this generation when they have grasped who Father is, will communicate His heart, His Grace and His healing, His desire to know and be known to their generation, and to ours in the imaginative, expressive, exuberant, over the top creative ways that express whose children they are, children of an extravagantly creator Father.

I believe that it is possible for small groups of new communities of this new generation to demonstrate that it is possible to be church and do church in a way that reflects Jacob and pleases the Father.

I believe that in the areas where it is necessary, that there are those in this generation who will be able to do the small counter-cultural things, that will affect others and thus create a mighty big avalanche of healthy change, and a restoration to the robbed.

I believe in this generation. Do you believe that, with the Father's help, joining in partnership with the creator, that they can change the Future?

Don't underestimate yourself, and definitely don't underestimate what God can do with you and through you. Be a change agent!